Our Identification with Christ's Sacrifice

Foreshadowed in the Old Testament Offerings

And Illustrated by Holy Communion

By

David Bergey

"Search the Scriptures, *John 5. 39. For they are they which testify of me:* the Scripture is the best Interpreter of itself. We cannot judge of these legal Shadows but by Scripture-light …Go no further than we see the Scripture going before us."

Mr. Samuel Mather, a sometime Pastor of a Church in Dublin, 1683

All Scriptures quoted are from the Authorized King James Version unless otherwise noted. Explanatory insertions within a scripture verse are enclosed in brackets. All Hebrew and Greek words are italicized and transliterated into English

Bold print in scripture quotations is emphasis added for teaching purposes only.

Our Identification with Christ's Sacrifice

Table of Contents

Preface

The point of this study of the Old Testament offerings is to see Jesus Christ and his finished work of redemption more clearly. The second intent is to help to unfold sections of the Church Epistles which pertain to sacrifices, especially that great sacrifice of Jesus Christ on our behalf.

Our main objective is to know Christ and what he has accomplished for us:

> Philippians 3:10:
> That I may know him, and the power of his resurrection, and the fellowship [*koinonia*, to share fully] of his sufferings, being made conformable unto his death;

This study's aim is to expand our appreciation of our "identification" or our spiritual union we have with Christ. If this topic of "identification with Christ" is new to you — or you feel you do not understand it adequately — I trust this study will help.

God revealed this identification to His people in the sacrifices and offerings of the Old Testament. Later, Jesus Christ set up Holy Communion, where we drink the wine and eat the bread, as a vivid object lesson of our identification or "common union" with him. We can live the power of God in our lives as we understand the reality of what Christ has done for us.

Hebrews 10:1-14

For the law having a shadow of good things to come, *and* not the very image of the things, can never with those sacrifices which they offered year by year continually make the comers thereunto perfect.

For then would they not have ceased to be offered? because that the worshippers once purged should have had no more conscience of sins.

But in those *sacrifices there is* a remembrance again *made* of sins every year.

For *it is* not possible that the blood of bulls and of goats should take away sins.

Wherefore when he cometh into the world, he saith, Sacrifice and offering thou wouldest not, but a body hast thou prepared me:

In burnt offerings and *sacrifices* for sin thou hast had no pleasure.

Then said I, Lo, I come (in the volume of the book it is written of me,) to do thy will, O God.

Above when he said, Sacrifice and offering and burnt offerings and *offering* for sin thou wouldest not, neither hadst pleasure *therein*; which are offered by the law;

Then said he, Lo, I come to do thy will, O God. He taketh away the first, that he may establish the second.

By the which will we are sanctified through the offering of the body of Jesus Christ once *for all*.

And every priest standeth daily ministering and offering oftentimes the same sacrifices, which can never take away sins:

But this man, after he had offered one sacrifice for sins for ever, sat down on the right hand of God;

From henceforth expecting till his enemies be made his footstool.

For by one offering he hath perfected for ever them that are sanctified.

Chapter One

"He Wrote of Me"

"The Old Testament is the New Testament concealed and the New Testament is the Old Testament revealed." When considering Jesus Christ and his work of redemption, this old saying often holds true. According to the New Testament, a very important key to interpreting and understanding the Old Testament is to examine it in light of Jesus Christ. Christ taught that the Old Testament Scriptures should be carefully searched because they testified of him.

> John 5:39 and 40:
> Search the scriptures; for in them ye think ye have eternal life: and they are they which testify of me.
> And ye will not come to me, that ye might have life.

Here Christ is teaching in the presence of unbelieving Judeans who sought to have him killed (John 5:16-18). When he said "search the scriptures," he was referring to the Old Testament writings. Of course, at the time he was speaking, what we call the "New Testament" had not yet been written. He continues this topic in verses 46 and 47:

> For had ye believed Moses, ye would have believed me: for he wrote of me.

"He Wrote of Me"

But if ye believe not his writings, how shall ye believe my words?

"...He [Moses] wrote of me." Where and how did Moses write of Christ? There is no need to speculate because so much of the answer to this is found in the New Testament itself. The New Testament reveals how and where Moses wrote of Christ. As we search the Gospels and the Epistles, we see many examples of how Moses wrote of Christ. For example, Hebrews 10 reveals that the sacrifices instituted by Moses are a "shadow" of the coming Christ.

In John 1 we have quite a refreshing contrast to the unbelievers spoken to in John 5.

John 1:45 and 46:
Philip findeth Nathanael, and saith unto him, We have found him, of whom Moses in the law, and the prophets, did write, Jesus of Nazareth, the son of Joseph.
And Nathanael said unto him, Can there any good thing come out of Nazareth? Philip saith unto him, Come and see.

Phillip's eyes were open to who Jesus of Nazareth was very early in his ministry. This verse in John pre-dates the great public miracles Christ starting in chapter 2. Yet Phillip believed. He had not yet seen the great public miracles, the crucifixion or the resurrection. But he was boldly sharing who Jesus was. Here was a young Galilean "on the cutting edge." This new disciple, who later became an apostle, was on the vanguard, in the forefront, witnessing that Jesus was the Messiah written about by Moses and the prophets. In sharp contrast, the Jerusalem bluebloods with Ph.D.s in "Old Testament Studies" sought to murder Jesus Christ despite all the great public signs and miracles he had done. These signs witnessed to his identity as the Messiah. The Jerusalem elders' eyes were blinded to who Jesus Christ was in spite of their vast knowledge of the Old Testament Scriptures.

Paul writes of the same problem that Christ confronted in the Gospel of John:

> II Corinthians 3:13-16:
> And not as Moses, *which* put a vail over his face, that the children of Israel could not stedfastly look **to the end of that which is abolished:**
> But their minds were blinded [hardened] for until this day remaineth the same vail untaken away in the reading of the old testament; which *vail* is done away in Christ.
> But even unto this day, when Moses is read, the vail is upon their heart.
> Nevertheless when it shall turn to the Lord, the vail shall be taken away.

In the reading of the Books of Moses, Genesis through Deuteronomy, a vail was upon the heart of the Judeans. They did not see that Moses wrote of Christ. II Corinthians 3:13 says exactly <u>what</u> their minds were blinded to: "that which is abolished." Verse 7 of this chapter parallels and clarifies verse 13:

> II Corinthians 3:7:
> But if the ministration of death, written *and* engraven in stones, was glorious, so that the children of Israel could not stedfastly behold the face of Moses for the glory of his countenance; which *glory* was to be done away [abolished].

When and how was the glory of the Old Covenant established by Moses abolished? It was abolished — annulled or voided — by the sacrificial work of Christ.

Ephesians 2:15:
Having abolished in his flesh the enmity, *even* the law of commandments *contained* in ordinances; for to make in himself of twain one new man, *so* making peace;

"...Abolished in his flesh" refers to the annulment of the old covenant law and its commandments by Christ's sacrifice of himself. Christ and his sacrificial work which abolished and ended the Law is <u>what</u> they did not see.

An examination of the Greek from which I Corinthians 3:13 is translated adds more light. It says they could not "stedfastly look to [*eis*] the end [*telos*] of that which was abolished." *Eis* means unto, with a view toward. This preposition "denotes motion *to* or *unto* an object, with the purpose of reaching or touching it."[1] *Telos* means the complete and full end. *Telos* is not merely cessation but fulfillment and completion.[2] What was the end or fulfillment of the Law that they could not see?

Romans 10:4 says that "Christ is the end [*telos*] of the law." Christ's sacrifice, the crucifixion, was the complete and full end, the *telos,* of that Old Testament law. Right before his death Christ said, "It is finished [*teleo*]" (John 19:30). His once and for all sacrifice voided and closed out the law. The end, the *telos,* of the Old Covenant is <u>what</u> they could not look unto. They could not see how Christ brought the whole law unto total completion and fulfillment by laying down his life at Calvary.

---

[1] The Companion Bible (London: Bagster, 1972) appendix 104.

[2] E. W. Bullinger, *Lexicon and Concordance* (London: Bagster, 1974) 248.

Their myopic gaze was not all the way unto, *eis*, the end of that which was abolished. Being shortsighted, their vision did not extend all the way unto the end of the law. They did not steadfastly look "unto the object" of the end of the law: Christ. Their eyes were blinded to Jesus Christ of Nazareth being written about by Moses. As we consider the Old Testament offerings in light of Christ revealed in the New Testament, the work of Christ on our behalf will be amplified in our understanding. We can behold with eyes uncovered and enlightened the finished work of Christ on our behalf.

The Old Testament Offerings Foreshadowed Christ

One of the ways Moses wrote of the coming Christ was in the Old Testament sacrifices and offerings. The sacrifices of the Old Testament present many parallels to the sacrifice of Christ. One common example of an Old Testament sacrifice with many parallels to the sacrifice of Christ is the Passover (Exodus 12). The New Testament reveals that Christ is our Passover (I Corinthians 5:7). The Gospels and the Epistles also reveal other parallels to the Passover sacrifice. All of the offerings of the Old Testament parallel or represent the coming Messiah and his work in some way.

The following verses speak of a "shadow of good things to come:"

Hebrews 9:28 and 10:1:
So Christ was once offered to bear the sins of many; and unto them that look for him shall he appear the second time without sin unto salvation.

For the law having a **shadow of good things to come**, *and* not the very image of the things, can never with those sacrifices which they offered year by year continually make the comers thereunto perfect.

These offerings under the law were a shadow, silhouette, an outline of that coming Messiah who would offer himself. Moses wrote of Christ as he instituted the Old Testament offerings by revelation from God. God foreknew Christ and therefore foreshadowed him in the offerings which Moses set up in the Law. These offerings as a "shadow of good things to come" pointed toward the coming Christ and his redemptive work on our behalf. These sacrifices found in the book of Leviticus were set up in anticipation of the true and perfect sacrifice of the body of Jesus Christ. Like an architect's blueprints, these Old Covenant sacrifices sketched out a detailed drawing of him who was to come.

Our Identification with Christ

One of the primary ways Christ was foreshadowed in the offerings was in the identification the Old Covenant believers had with animal sacrifices. We will examine the Mosaic offerings and then see how God uses Holy Communion as an illustration to help us recognize and realize our identification with Christ. By drinking the wine and eating the bread in Holy Communion, God has given a vivid object lesson to remind us of our full sharing and utter oneness we have with our Lord and Savior, Jesus Christ. This identification with Christ is vividly set forth in Galatians 2:20:

I am [was] crucified with Christ: nevertheless I live; yet not I, but Christ liveth in me: and the life which I now live in the flesh I live by the faith of the Son of God, who loved me, and gave himself for me.

"Am" should be "was." This is not something you do daily. It was done in Christ. This is not something you <u>do</u>; it was <u>done</u>! By our identification with Christ we have shared fully in his suffering, his death and his resurrection. God has made us utterly one with Christ in the new birth.

When I was first taught this verse and others relating to my identification with my Savior, Jesus Christ, it was a brand new concept to my mind. It seemed a sparkling new revelation laid out for the first time in the seven Church epistles. From my church background I knew "Jesus Saved." I had heard he died in my place, as a substitute. But this idea of identification with Christ was an idea unheard of, much less understood, much less ever lived and applied. However, as my understanding of this topic matured, it became apparent that this concept of the believers' identification with Christ was one that God has been diligently endeavoring to communicate to His people throughout the ages.

As we shall see, this concept of identification is intrinsic, built in, inherent to the Old Testament sacrifices. When that sacrifice brought by the Old Covenant believer died, all his sin died with it. Thus, the offering was "identified" with the offerer. That is, the life of that animal and the life of that Old Covenant believer became <u>identical</u> in a legal sense in the sight of God. For this reason, the lifeblood of the offering was shed on behalf of the life of the offerer.

Our identification with the Savior is not a narrow, obscure topic that only the completely initiated, elite brains, could ever understand. God has been trying to communicate this subject to every believer, repeatedly, by way of the Scriptures. God has desired His people to grasp the idea of their identification, their utter oneness, their full sharing with Christ. In this identification, all sin and penalties for sin are transferred to Christ, our substitute. Hence, he bears the penalty, death, so we do not have to. Since the penalty of sin, death, was transferred to our substitute, we can freely approach God.

We can come before the presence of God because all our sin, all our inadequacy to worship God, to approach God, has been taken care of. All of our sin has been transferred to an innocent substitute, who was without spot or blemish. In the death of this substitute, all the claims of a just and perfect God have been satisfied.

II Corinthians 5:21:
For He hath **made** him to be sin for us, who knew no sin; that we might be **made** the righteousness of God in him.

Here we have a transfer of our sin **to** him, and God's righteousness **to** us. A more accurate translation would be: "For God hath made him to be a sin offering for us." The word "offering" should be supplied. As a sin offering all our sin was transferred to him. In this sense we have been "crucified with Christ." This is our full sharing with Christ.

God has made a consistent effort to reveal and clarify the great truth of identification or full sharing with Christ in His Word. Here are some of the illustrations utilized in Scripture to communicate our oneness with Christ, our identification with him:

1. The vine and the branches (John 15)
2. The bridegroom and the bride (Ephesians 5)
3. The head of the body and members of the body. (Ephesians 2 and 3)

4. "Surety" meaning guarantor or "co-signer" (Hebrews 7:22). Genesis 43 illustrates Christ as "surety" by a historical event: Judah is surety for Benjamin; big brother offers his life for little brother.
5. Baptism (Romans 6:1-4)
6. Holy Communion

These are different illustrations in different contexts with different facets. But all have one great truth: our identification with Christ; our full sharing with him, our utter oneness with him. The subject of identification is one great gem in God's Word with many refracting, glistening facets.

Chapter Two

Identification
in the Levitical Offerings

Laying the Hand on the Head of the Sacrifice

God's ongoing attempt to communicate this great truth of identification goes back to the offerings of Leviticus given under Law as well as before the Law. In Leviticus, chapters 1-7, five different offerings are set forth. Leviticus 7:37 summarizes these five offerings:

> Leviticus 7:37:
> This is the law of the burnt offering, of the meat offering, and of the sin offering, and of the trespass offering, and of the consecrations, and of the sacrifices of the peace offerings.

This is a listing of these offerings instituted under the Law in Leviticus 1-7:
1. Burnt Offering
2. Meat (meal) Offering
3. Peace Offering
4. Sin Offering
5. Trespass Offering

Our Identification with Christ's Sacrifice

These five offerings are patterns or illustrations or shadows of Jesus Christ who would lay down his life as that "once for all" offering. With this in mind, let us look at one of the activities done in connection with the Old Testament sacrifices.

> Leviticus 1:1-5:
> And the Lord called unto Moses, and spake unto him out of the tabernacle of the congregation, saying,
> Speak unto the children of Israel and say unto them, If any man of you bring an offering unto the Lord, ye shall bring your offering of the cattle, even of the herd, and of the flock.
> If his offering be a burnt sacrifice of the herd, let him offer a male lamb without blemish: he shall offer it of his own voluntary will at the door of the tabernacle of the congregation before the Lord.
> v. 4: And he shall **put his hand upon the head** of the burnt offering; and it shall be accepted for him to make atonement for him. (emphasis added)
> And he shall kill the bullock before the Lord, and the priests, Aaron's sons, shall bring the blood, and sprinkle the blood round about upon the altar that is by the door of the tabernacle of the congregation.

In verse four the offerer placed "his hand upon the head of the burnt offering." This expressed identification with that innocent offering which was "without blemish." Placing the hand on the head of the sacrifice signified a transfer, identifying the offering with the offerer. The offering was then presented as a substitute to God. The burnt offering represented the whole life of the offerer being given to God, totally and completely. God then accepted this offering as a sweet savour, a pleasing aroma (v. 9, 13, 17).

16

Identification in the Levitical Offerings

The action of the offerer laying his hands on the head of the offering foreshadows the believer's identification with Christ. Laying a hand on the head of the offering represents a "full sharing" with that sacrifice. This gesture identified the offerer with the sacrifice, transferring all the sin and inadequacy of the offerer to the offering and the innocence of the sacrifice to the offerer.

E.W Bullinger has a noteworthy comment in his Companion Bible on Leviticus 1:4 encapsulating this truth we are looking at:

> There was a double transfer: the unworthiness of the offerer was transferred to the victim; and the acceptableness of the offering was transferred to the offerer.

Remember II Corinthians 5:21? "For He hath made him to be sin for us, who knew no sin; that we might be made the righteousness of God in him." Here there is this double transfer. Our sin is transferred to him and righteousness is transferred to us.

The same heart of God pulses through these Old Testament verses that pulses in Ephesians and Romans. But the average modern reader often looks at these sacrifices in Leviticus as some ancient cryptic rite with as much relevance to him as soil samples from Mars.

Leviticus 3:1, 2, 8, 13:
And if his oblation [offering] be a sacrifice for peace offering, if he offer it of the herd; whether it be a male or female, he shall offer it without blemish before the Lord. And he shall **lay his hand upon the head** of his offering
...

v. 8: And he shall **lay his hand upon the head** of his
offering and kill it before the tabernacle...
v. 13: And he shall **lay his hand upon the head** of it and
kill it before the tabernacle...

With the peace offerings, the hand of the offerer was also
laid on the head of the sacrifice, demonstrating
identification.

Leviticus 4:4, 15, 24, 29, 33:
v. 4: ... and shall lay his hand upon the bullock's head...
v. 15:...shall lay their hands upon the head of the bullock
before the Lord...
v. 24: ...and he shall lay his hand upon the head of the
goat...
v. 29: ...And he shall lay his hand upon the head of the
sin offering...
v. 33: ...And he shall lay his hand upon the head of the
sin offering...

With the sin offering the offering also stood as a substitute
for the offerer and identification with the offerer. Or as
Bullinger put it, a "double transfer," — the sin of the offerer
being transferred to the innocent sacrifice and the innocence
of the sacrifice being transferred to the offerer:

This act of laying the hand on the head of the offering was
central to these various offerings in Leviticus. Time and time
again it is mentioned as an integral part of sacrifice. The
offerer was identified with the offering by this act,
foreshadowing our identification with our Lord and Savior,
Jesus Christ, in the new birth.

Another example of identification and substitution in the offerings is on the Day of Atonement. A "public" sacrifice was performed by the high priest for the whole nation. In Leviticus 1-7 "private" sacrifices were brought by and for the individual. On the Day of Atonement the high priest transferred the sins of the nation to the animal by laying his hands on the animal.

> Leviticus 16:21 and 22:
> And Aaron shall **lay both his hands upon the head** of the live goat, and confess over him all the iniquities of the children of Israel, and all their transgressions in all their sins, **putting them upon the head of the goat**, and shall send *him* away by the hand of a fit man into the wilderness:
> And **the goat shall bear upon him all their iniquities** unto a land not inhabited: and he shall let go the goat in the wilderness.

Could God make it any plainer? Could He spell it out any clearer? As the scapegoat is taken away so all the sins are taken away. This innocent animal carried away all the sins with him. The sins of the people were transferred to this innocent animal.

Eating the Sacrifice

Another way our identification with Christ was foreshadowed in the offerings is in the eating of the offerings as a sacrificial meal. The offering was slain and prepared and the family and friends would share in a meal eating the sacrifice. Eating of the sacrifice together represented a full sharing with the sacrifice and with each other. Because of this identification with the sacrifice, the sacrificial meal signified union with God and communion with each other.

Our Identification with Christ's Sacrifice

This sacrificial meal was an integral part of both the peace offering and the Passover offering. The idea of a sacrificial meal will come up again when we look at I Corinthians 10 and 11.

In Exodus 12 Israel signified this identification by eating the Passover lamb:

> Exodus 12:6-11:
> And ye shall keep it up until the fourteenth day of the same month: and the whole
> assembly of the congregation of Israel shall kill it in the evening.
> And they shall take of the blood, and strike *it* on the two side posts and on the upper door post of the houses, wherein they shall eat it.
> And they shall eat the flesh in that night, roast with fire, and unleavened bread; *and* with bitter *herbs* they shall eat it.
> Eat not of it raw, nor sodden at all with water, but roast *with* fire; his head with his legs, and with the purtenance thereof.
> And ye shall let nothing of it remain until the morning; and that which remaineth of it until the morning ye shall burn with fire.
> And thus shall ye eat it; *with* your loins girded, your shoes on your feet, and your staff in your hand; and ye shall eat it in haste: it *is* the LORD'S passover.

Israel was to completely consume the sacrifice; to partake fully of the Passover. Eating the sacrifice represented a full sharing with that sacrifice. This foreshadowed our full sharing in Christ's sacrifice and all that it accomplished for us.

The ingesting of the flesh of the Passover lamb was a precursor of the full sharing and complete union with the coming Messiah. This lamb without spot or blemish had died in Israel's place. All the sin, sickness and death was transferred to this innocent lamb. Consequently, God's deliverance, God's wholeness and forgiveness were conveyed to them. The Passover lamb stood as a substitute before God just as Christ would. I Corinthians 5:7 states: "... Christ our Passover is sacrificed for us."

Identification illustrated in the Old Testament Sacrifices:

1. Laying a hand on the head of the sacrifice
2. Eating the sacrifice

We have expressions: "a picture is worth a 1000 words" and "do I have to draw you a picture?" God did that for us in His Word. What wonderful illustrations, portraits and sketches God made in the Old Testament of this aspect of the coming Messiah. He demonstrated time after time the concept of transfer; or as it has been called, substitution and identification.

Chapter Three

Holy Communion

How does God illustrate this idea of identification since the coming of Christ? How does He explain this essential concept of the sacrificial work of Christ to us? What has He set up to communicate this knowledge of identification and substitution to us?

God has done it by what we call "Holy Communion" or as it is also called, "the Lord's Supper." "Communion" is made up of two words, common and union. We have "common union" or identification with Christ. The Greek word for communion is *koinonia* meaning to share fully.

As we shall see, when we eat the bread and drink the wine, it illustrates our full sharing, our identification with Christ in his sacrifice. It portrays this idea of transference we have between Christ and us in his sacrifice. In both the Gospels and the Epistles the communion service is set forth as a vivid object lesson of our full sharing, our "common-union," our identification with Christ.

Meal and Drink Offerings Illustrate Christ in the Old Testament as Holy Communion does in the New Testament

Before examining Holy Communion in the Gospels and the Epistles, it would help our understanding to see how frequently bread and wine were used in the sacrifices of the Old Testament. Using bread and wine to represent the body and blood of Christ is not unique to the New Testament. Albeit in the Old Testament, the offerings of bread and wine foreshadowed Christ while in the New Testament the bread and wine of Communion look back on Christ in remembrance. The Old Testament sacrifice of bread or meal was called the "meat offering" in the King James Version. The sacrifice of wine was called the "drink offering." The meal and drink offering were prevalent among the Old Testament sacrifices.

In Numbers 28 the required daily sacrifices of the priests were spelled out in detail.

> Numbers 28:3 and 4:
> And thou shalt say unto them, This *is* the offering made by fire which ye shall offer unto the LORD; two lambs of the first year without spot day by day, *for* a continual burnt offering.
> The one lamb shalt thou offer in the morning, and the other lamb shalt thou offer at even;

These daily offerings were not to be done just once a day, but twice, in the morning and "even." God ordained this sacrifice to be done twice a day, every day, so His people would have a constant portrayal of the great sacrifice of he who was to come. Hebrews 10:11 mentions the daily sacrifices of the Old Covenant priests.

Hebrews 10:11 and 12:
And every priest standeth daily ministering and offering oftentimes the same sacrifices, which can never take away sins:
But this man, after he had offered one sacrifice for sins for ever, sat down on the right hand of God;

The constant, daily sacrifices of the Old Testament priests are compared to the one-time, complete sacrifice of Christ. These daily sacrifices performed a valuable function of looking forward to and portraying the coming Christ and his sacrificial work on our behalf.

Numbers 28:5-8:
And a tenth *part* of an ephah of flour for a **meat [meal] offering**, mingled with the fourth *part* of an hin of beaten oil.
It is a continual burnt offering, which was ordained in mount Sinai for a sweet savour, a sacrifice made by fire unto the LORD.
And the **drink offering** thereof *shall be* the fourth *part* of an hin for the one lamb: in the holy *place* shalt thou cause the strong wine to be poured unto the LORD *for* a **drink offering**.
And the other lamb shalt thou offer at even: as the **meat [meal] offering** of the morning, and as the **drink offering** thereof, thou shalt offer *it*, a sacrifice made by fire, of a sweet savour unto the LORD.

The meal and drink offerings were an integral and important part of the daily offerings made by the priests. As verse 7 says, the drink offerings were not drunk by the priests but poured out. The vital significance of these the meal and drink offerings extended to the entire system of sacrifices and offerings instituted by Moses under the Law. Besides the daily offerings, the Sabbath days, new moons and feast days called for repeated offerings of bread and wine.

For example, in the book of Numbers alone, there are at least 25 specific references to the meal and drink offerings being offered in conjunction with each other. (Numbers 6:15-17; 15:1-10, 24; 28:5-14, 31; 29:6, 11, 16, 18, 19, 21, 22, 24, 25, 27, 28, 30, 33-39). The combination of the meal and drink offerings were widespread under the Old Covenant.

As was often the case, these offerings were combined with an animal sacrifice. In the daily offering are the three prominent symbols of the sacrificial work of Christ in the New Testament: Christ as the lamb of God and the bread and wine as used in Holy Communion. The offering of the lamb, meal offering and drink offering were to be offered together, foreshadowing the coming Messiah and the accomplishment of his once-and-for-all sacrifice for God's people.

Before the Law, in Genesis 14 there is another example of the offering of bread and the wine foreshadowing Christ. In this account a confederation of kings attacked and plundered the wicked city of Sodom taking its food, goods and captives. One of the captives was Lot, a relative of the great believer, Abram (later named Abraham). Abram attacked the army of the kings and defeated it. After the victory Abram was met by Melchizedek, a priest of the Most High God.

Genesis 14:18 and 19:

Our Identification with Christ's Sacrifice

> And Melchizedek king of Salem brought forth bread and wine: and he *was* the priest of the most high God.
>
> And he blessed him, and said, Blessed *be* Abram of the most high God, possessor of heaven and earth:

Some scholars say this bread and wine is "food-aid" for Abram and his hungry troops.[3] Yet, it is clear from the context that there was no need to feed Abram and his men. Genesis 14:11 states food was a prime part of the booty taken from Sodom, which was later re-captured by Abram's men. Also, the final verse of the chapter shows that Abram's men had indeed helped themselves to this food which had belonged to Sodom. So, if Melchizedek was not bringing this bread and wine to relieve hunger and thirst, what was its purpose?

This bread and wine was an offering to God. Melchizedek was acting in his capacity as "the priest of the most high God," presenting the bread and the wine as an offering to God. Whether Melchizedek or Abram consumed the offering or if it was offered in some other way is not stated here in Genesis. But, what is important for our understanding is that, first, it was an offering and second, that it represented the coming Christ. Here the bread and the wine foreshadowed Christ, looking forward in anticipation to his sacrifice. The bread and wine of Holy Communion looks back in remembrance to the sacrifice of Christ.

In Genesis the full significance of Melchizedek is not immediately apparent. In Hebrew chapter six and seven, however, over 20 verses are spent on Melchizedek. Hebrews

---

[3] C.F. Keil and R. Delitzsch, *Commentary on the Old Testament* (Grand Rapids, Michigan: Eeerdmans, reprinted 1986) Volume I, 207.

6:20 states of Christ, "thou art a priest forever after the manner of Melchisedec..." Melchizedek is no biblical lightweight. Just as Melchizedek presented an offering bread and wine, Jesus Christ presented his own flesh and his own blood as a sacrifice on our behalf.

In conclusion, the meal and drink offerings of the Old Testament represented or foreshadowed the flesh and blood of Christ sacrificed on our behalf. These offerings combined to form a wonderful complement, portraying the sacrifice of Christ. The meal offering corresponded to the flesh of Christ, while the drink offering of wine corresponded to the blood of Christ. What a lovely depiction of the coming redeemer these offerings formed! The Holy Communion instituted by Christ in the New Testament as a remembrance of what Christ accomplished, directly and uniquely parallels the meal and drink offerings of the Old Testament.

Jesus Christ Institutes Holy Communion

In the Gospel of John, some months previous to instituting Holy Communion, Jesus attempted to convey a truth which formed the core and the essence of Holy Communion. He explained, by two vivid illustrations the identification, the full sharing, he, the Messiah would have with the believers. As we will read, misunderstanding of this very important point caused great bewilderment in many of Christ's disciples.

Here in John 6, Jesus refers back to the time of Moses when God fed the children of Israel with manna when they were in the wilderness for forty years.

John 6:32-33; 47-52:

Then Jesus said unto them, Verily, verily, I say unto you,
Moses gave you not that bread from heaven; but my
Father giveth you the true bread from heaven.
For the bread of God is he which cometh down from
heaven, and giveth life unto the world…
…Verily, verily, I say unto you, He that believeth on me
hath everlasting life.
I am that bread of life.
Your fathers did eat manna in the wilderness, and are
dead.
This is the bread which cometh down from heaven, that a
man may eat thereof, and not die.
I am the living bread which came down from heaven: if
any man eat of this bread, he shall live for ever: and the
bread that I will give is my flesh, which I will give for the
life of the world.
The Jews therefore strove among themselves, saying,
How can this man give us *his* flesh to eat?

Jesus said he was the true bread from heaven that gives life
unto the world. He uses the manna to illustrate the eternal
life he would give to the world. But the Jews questioned his
meaning. Even though they missed his point he continued
his explanation in even more depth, shifting to another
illustration.

John 6:53-57:
Then Jesus said unto them, Verily, verily, I say unto you,
Except ye eat the flesh of the Son of man, and drink his
blood, ye have no life in you.
Whoso eateth my flesh and drinketh my blood, hath
eternal life; and I will raise him up at the last day.
For my flesh is meat indeed, and my blood is drink
indeed;

He that eateth my flesh and drinketh my blood, dwelleth in me, and I in him.
As the living Father hath sent me, and I live by the Father: so he that eateth me, even he shall live by me.

The mention of "eating my flesh and drinking my blood" of verses 53-57 is an abrupt shift from equating his body with manna as he did previously in the passage. Now he is looking forward to "Holy Communion" which he would institute a few months later. Either way, his point remained the same: the identification of the believers with Christ. Jesus was saying: Just as your fathers ingested the manna from God and lived, so you must ingest me to get eternal life.

To understand this passage, one needs to remember a biblical idiom. To eat means to ingest inwardly; to receive within, not necessarily a physical eating, but a mental or spiritual ingestion.

Jeremiah 15:16:
Thy words were found, and I did eat them; and thy word was unto me the joy and rejoicing of mine heart: for I am called by thy name, O LORD God of hosts.

We need to understand this passage in John in light of this idiom. But there is also a deeper truth to consider. In the "eating of his flesh" he is alluding back to the Passover sacrifice and other sacrifices that were eaten, as well as the manna. They ate the flesh of the Passover sacrifice. This very year he spoke these words, Jesus Christ was to be the Passover sacrifice for all time.

This imagery of drinking the blood and eating the flesh was later carried over into the "Communion." When we understand what Communion represents, we can fully grasp what he was getting at in John 6. At the heart of his message is a spiritual ingestion of all that Christ is—into every believer. Jesus is teaching about the full sharing, an utter oneness, the full unity every believer would have with Christ once he laid down his life as the once and for all sacrifice for all time.

Now Christ switches back to the illustration of manna, which he had used previously in the chapter:

> John 6:58-66:
> This is that bread which came down from heaven: not as your fathers did eat manna, and are dead: he that eateth of this bread shall live for ever.
> These things said he in the synagogue, as he taught in Capernaum.
> Many therefore of his disciples, when they had heard this, said, This is a hard saying;
> who can hear it?
> When Jesus knew in himself that his disciples murmured at it, he said unto them, Doth this offend you?
> *What* and if ye shall see the Son of man ascend up where he was before?
> It is the spirit that quickeneth; the flesh profiteth nothing: the words that I speak unto you, *they* are spirit, and *they* are life.
> But there are some of you that believe not. For Jesus knew from the beginning who they were that believed not, and who should betray him.
> And he said, Therefore said I unto you, that no man can come unto me, except it were given unto him of my Father.
> From that *time* many of his disciples went back, and walked no more with him.

Holy Communion

Many of his disciples didn't understand. This vital truth of their full identification with the Messiah was completely missed. Here Christ was trying to illustrate and to explain the believers' identification and full sharing **with him**. He was teaching, with little immediate success, how there would be a full sharing, an utter oneness, an identification with him by the coming new birth.

Jesus Christ didn't give up! He did not stop teaching this great and vital truth just because they didn't understand here in John 6. Some months later he set this truth forth again. He drove it home one more time. This time he picked an hour and a day that no one there could ever forget. This is what is called the last supper. Right after this meal he would be betrayed and then crucified. This scene would be etched on their memories for the rest of their lives.

> Matthew 26:26-31:
> And as they were eating, Jesus took bread, and blessed *it*, and brake *it*, and gave *it* to the disciples, and said, Take, eat; this is my body.
> And he took the cup, and gave thanks, and gave *it* to them, saying, Drink ye all of it;
> For this is my blood of the new testament, which is shed for many for the remission of sins.
> But I say unto you, I will not drink henceforth of this fruit of the vine, until that day when I drink it new with you in my Father's kingdom.
> And when they had sung an hymn, they went out into the mount of Olives.
> Then saith Jesus unto them, All ye shall be offended because of me this night: for it is written, I will smite the shepherd, and the sheep of the flock shall be scattered abroad.

Christ instituted a vivid object lesson of the full sharing, the identification, the believers would have with his sacrifice at Calvary.

Our Identification with Christ Illustrated by Holy Communion in I Corinthians 10 and 11

Years later, Paul writes to the Corinthians and by God's revelation reiterates the importance of and gives more explanation about Holy Communion. While I Corinthians 10 and 11 reprove idolatry and other practical errors, a fundamental, underlying theme in these chapters is our identification with Christ.

> I Corinthians 10:1 and 2:
> Moreover, brethren, I would not that ye should be ignorant, how that all our fathers were under the cloud, and all passed through the sea;
> And were all baptized unto Moses in the cloud and in the sea;

In the Exodus from Egypt, Moses led them through the cloud and the sea. Israel was fully immersed into all that Moses believed God to bring to pass for them. As they were identified with Moses, so we are identified with Christ. We share fully in all that Christ has accomplished for us.

> I Corinthians 10:3 and 4:
> And did all eat the same spiritual meat [manna];
> And did all drink the same spiritual drink: for they drank of that spiritual Rock that followed them: and that Rock was Christ.

Holy Communion

What great truth is being set forth here? They ate the manna and they drank from the rock. Both represented Christ. In John 6, Jesus also stated that he was the true bread from heaven. The big point here, as well as in John 6, is identification with Christ.

This chapter opens with a passionate declaration: "I would not that ye should be ignorant..." Ignorant of what? Their full immersion into Christ, their utter oneness, their complete union with Christ—or as we have called it—identification with Christ. But how ignorant or unmindful the Christian Church has been concerning this topic. Here in His Word, God is making an effort to reveal and clarify our identification with Christ, utilizing illustrations from the Old Testament.

I Corinthians 10:5-15:
But with many of them God was not well pleased: for they were overthrown in the wilderness.
Now these things were our examples, to the intent we should not lust after evil things, as they also lusted.
Neither be ye idolaters, as *were* some of them; as it is written, The people sat down to eat and drink, and rose up to play.
Neither let us commit fornication, as some of them committed, and fell in one day three and twenty thousand.
Neither let us tempt Christ, as some of them also tempted, and were destroyed of serpents.
Neither murmur ye, as some of them also murmured, and were destroyed of the destroyer.
Now all these things happened unto them for ensamples: and they are written for our admonition, upon whom the ends of the world are come.

Wherefore let him that thinketh he standeth take heed lest he fall.

There hath no temptation taken you but such as is common to man: but God *is* faithful, who will not suffer you to be tempted above that ye are able; but will with the temptation also make a way to escape, that ye may be able to bear *it*.

Wherefore, my dearly beloved, flee from idolatry.

I speak as to wise men; judge ye what I say.

While this chapter has many lessons, it returns to our identification with Christ in verse 16, this time in the context of Holy Communion:

I Corinthians 10:16:
The cup of blessing which we bless, is it not the communion [*koinonia*, sharing fully] of the blood of Christ? The bread which we break, is it not the communion [*koinonia*] of the body of Christ?

What does the wine represent in the Communion? A full sharing—*koinonia*—and identification **with** the blood of Christ. What does the bread represent as it is eaten in remembrance of Christ's sacrifice? A full sharing—*koinonia*—identification **with** the body of Christ. This is the crux, my main assertion, of this study. Holy Communion illustrates our identification with Christ.

I Corinthians 10:17:
For we *being* many are one bread, *and* one body: for we are all partakers [*metecho*], full sharing, full participation] of that one bread.

The "one bread" is Christ as mentioned in verses 3 and 4 and John 6. We all share fully in him. The verse should read:

34

"Because there is one loaf, we, although many, are one body, for we all partake of that one bread." *Metecho* is very similar to *koinonia*, meaning: full partnership, full participation. Here, once again, our spiritual union, our identification with Christ is the big point of this verse.

> I Corinthians 10:18:
> Behold Israel after the flesh: are not they which eat of the sacrifices partakers [*koinōnos*] of the altar?

This rhetorical question is at the crux of our earlier discussion on Old Testament sacrifices. Those that ate of the sacrifices shared fully with the altar. The altar represented the sacrifices offered on it. <u>In these Old Testament sacrifices there was a full sharing, an identification by way of transference which is inherent in sacrifice.</u>

In like manner, with the sacrifice of Christ there is also an identification with his great offering and all of its accomplishments. We share fully in that sacrifice. Now we need to walk out in faith to apply this reality.

> I Corinthians 10:19-21:
> What say I then? that the idol is any thing, or that which is offered in sacrifice to idols is any thing?
> But I *say*, that the things which the Gentiles sacrifice, they sacrifice to devils, and not to God: and I would not that ye should have fellowship [*koinonia*] with devils.
> Ye cannot drink the cup of the Lord, and the cup of devils: ye cannot be partakers [*metecho*] of the Lord's table, and of the table of devils.

Here the Apostle Paul presents exactly what occurs when the Gentiles sacrifice to their idols. These sacrifices they offer are to devil spirits represented by the idols. Also, eating and drinking these sacrifices offered to devil spirits symbolizes a full sharing [*koinonia*]. The intent of eating and drinking these sacrifices was to identify, to share with idols, or—as the Apostle candidly says—devils. Incidentally, there is evidence in other sources outside the Scriptures that eating the sacrifices was commonly understood to signify a sharing or identifying with the idol. (See appendix)

> I Corinthians 10:22-26:
> Do we provoke the Lord to jealousy? are we stronger than he?
> All things are lawful for me, but all things are not expedient [profitable]: all things are lawful for me, but all things edify not.
> Let no man seek his own, but every man another's *wealth* [profit--not "wealth"].
> Whatsoever is sold in the shambles [marketplace], *that* eat, asking no question for conscience sake:
> For the earth *is* the Lord's, and the fulness thereof.

The city of Corinth was awash in idolatry. Temples to the various Greek gods were plentiful. Festivals and feasts with food that had been sacrificed or dedicated to the gods were common. Often the food from the temples, which had been sacrificed to the deities, was sold in the marketplaces. In fact, a map of Corinth from this era shows the marketplaces were situated across from the temples.[4]

> I Corinthians 10:27-29:
> If any of them that believe not bid you *to a feast*, and ye be disposed to go; whatsoever is set before you, eat, asking no question for conscience sake.

---

[4] David Williams, *Paul's Metaphors, Their Context and Character* (Peabody, Mass.: Hendrickson, 1999) 29.

Holy Communion

But if any man say unto you, This is offered in sacrifice unto idols, eat not for his sake that shewed it, and for conscience sake: for the earth *is* the Lord's, and the fulness thereof:
Conscience, I say, not thine own, but of the other: for why is my liberty judged of another *man's* conscience?

When you eat food sacrificed and dedicated to an idol, you are spiritually identifying and sharing with that idol. This goes back to a common understanding in ancient times as we show in the appendix. However, the next verse indicates the way to negate this:

I Corinthians 10:30 and 31:
For if I by grace [thanksgiving] be a partaker, why am I evil spoken of for that for which I give thanks? Whether therefore ye eat, or drink, or whatsoever ye do, do all to the glory of God.

Before you eat, dedicate your food to God and give thanks. By blessing the food, to the glory of God, any negatives are superseded.

In chapter eleven of I Corinthians more explanation is given on Holy Communion.

I Corinthians 11:23-26:
For I have received [by revelation] of the Lord that which also I delivered unto you, That the Lord Jesus the *same* night in which he was betrayed took bread:
And when he had given thanks, he brake *it*, and said, Take, eat: this is my body, which is broken for you: this do in remembrance of me.
After the same manner also *he took* the cup, when he had supped, saying, This cup is the new testament in my

blood: this do ye, as oft as ye drink *it*, in remembrance of me.

For as often as ye eat this bread, and drink this cup, ye do shew [proclaim, declare] the Lord's death till he come.

This last verse is key to understanding the purpose of Holy Communion. By eating the bread and drinking the wine you proclaim and declare the Lord's death. Thayer's *Lexicon* says this word carries a sense of openly praising and celebrating as it proclaims.

What precisely is declared or proclaimed about his death? It is our common union with Christ, our identification with him in his sacrifice. As with the Old Testament sacrifices, there was a double transfer. All our sins were transferred to Christ and all his righteousness was transferred to us. Eating the bread and drinking the wine celebrates and reminds us of this reality. It proclaims our full sharing with our redeemer in his sacrifice for us.

As Galatians 2:20 says, "..."I was crucified with Christ." We were identified with him. As we keep our identification with Christ in full view, we can stop living with a strong sense of how little we measure up to what God has called us to. Our Lord and Savior has taken our place, he was crucified for us.

I Corinthians 11:27:
Wherefore whosoever shall eat this bread, and drink *this* cup of the Lord, unworthily [without discriminating and recognizing with due appreciation], shall be guilty of the body and blood of the Lord.

"Guilty" means to be held liable, to be legally subject to consequences.[5] In the Gospels it is translated, "in danger of judgment." Each person eating the bread and drinking the cup is fully responsible to understand the significance, to recognize with due appreciation, what it represents. When you forget the meaning of the cup and bread, you are culpable, not God, for the lack of results in your life.

> I Corinthians 11:28:
> But let a man examine **himself**, and so let him eat of *that* bread, and drink of *that* cup.

This verse does **not** say: "Let one man examine another man, and so don't let him eat."

> I Corinthians 11:29 and 30:
> For he that eateth and drinketh unworthily, eateth and drinketh damnation [judgement] to himself, not discerning [properly evaluating] the Lord's body.
> For this cause many *are* weak and sickly among you, and many sleep.

Again, as in verse 27, a more accurate rendering of "unworthily" (from *The Amplified Bible*) is "without discriminating and recognizing with due appreciation."

In these two verses emerge the core problem and its corresponding negative consequence. The Corinthian's practical error was not "discerning" the Lord's body. "Discerning" is the Greek *diakrino* meaning to separate, discriminate, distinguish, or make a distinction. It is translated "discerning" the sky to distinguish the varying weather conditions in Matthew 16:3. Wuest translates "discerning" as "properly evaluate."[6] They were <u>not</u>

---

[5] Joseph Henry Thayer, *Greek-English Lexicon of the New Testament* (Milford, MI: Baker House, 1977), 219.

distinguishing or discerning the significance of the Lord's body. They were oblivious, forgetful or ignorant of the specific details of the meaning of Christ's sacrifice on our behalf.

The negative consequence was physical weakness leading to sickness and premature death. In this instance many were unmindful that the sacrifice of Christ bore their sicknesses as well as their sins. As we shall see, one of the specifics of Christ's sacrifice for us was the transfer of both our sins and our sickness to him. It appears that many of the Corinthians had failed to make that distinction. They did not discern the fine details of exactly what the bread represented and what the wine represented. This was the bottleneck in manifesting what God had made available for them.

To live the reality of Christ's offering for us, in the here and now, precise knowledge of what he accomplished is crucial. If we lack discernment of what Communion represents, we won't share in the benefits. Since a superficial acceptance of some vague generalities of Holy Communion do not bring the results God intends, let's consider exactly what our identification, our union with Christ, has achieved for us.

---

[6] Kenneth Wuest, *The New Testament, An Expanded Translation* (Grand Rapids, Michigan: Eerdmans, 1961) 404.

Chapter Four

Living the Reality
of Christ's Offering

Manifesting the great truth of Christ's sacrificial work on our behalf is a matter of filling our thinking with the reality of precisely what he has accomplished for us. There is power in believing the specifics of what Christ accomplished from the Word of God.

> I Corinthians 1:18:
> For the preaching [*logos*, word] of the cross is to them that perish foolishness; but unto us which are saved it is the power of God.

The "word of the cross" is the knowledge of what Jesus Christ accomplished for us when he laid down his life as a sacrifice on our behalf. This "word of the cross" is for us the power of God. Living the reality of Christ's offering is to claim the mental and physical wholeness that we have in Christ.

> Matthew 8:16 and 17:
> When the even was come, they brought unto him many that were possessed with devils: and he cast out the spirits with *his* word, and healed all that were sick:

Our Identification with Christ's Sacrifice

> That it might be fulfilled which was spoken by Esaias the prophet, saying, Himself took [away] our infirmities, and bare [carried away] *our* sicknesses.

The literal text in Matthew is that Christ took **away** our infirmities and carried **away** our sickness. Get the vivid picture of the Old Testament sacrifice. After the offerer laid his hand on it; the priest led it away. As it was led away to the altar to be killed, all the sin and all the guilt of the believer was being taken away as well. Also, as the scapegoat was being led off into the wilderness, all the sins of the people were carried off, borne by the scapegoat. When that sacrifice goes — what else went with it? Your sins, your sickness, all your weakness and inadequacy to approach and serve God was taken away.

This animal sacrifice did not in and of itself take away sins. It represented, it symbolized the coming Savior who would actually take away sins. By believing, the Old Testament believers were to look <u>forward</u> to the coming redeemer through the sacrifices. In a similar way, in the Holy Communion we, as New Testament believers, look <u>backward</u> to the finished work of Christ. If we don't "discern," recognize with due appreciation, or properly evaluate all that the bread and wine represent, we don't get the results. In like manner, when the believers in the Old Testament failed to recognize the true meaning and significance of the sacrifices they did not see the results God intended.

Matthew 8:17 is quoting from Isaiah 53. This chapter in Isaiah is not a foreshadowing or representation of the coming Christ, but a direct and detailed explanation of the coming Savior. In this section of Isaiah we see a direct prophecy of the coming Savior and his sacrificial work. This suffering servant will voluntarily lay down his life as a sacrificial offering to bare the sins of mankind.

Isaiah 52:13-15:
Behold, my servant shall deal prudently, he shall be exalted and extolled, and be very high.
As many were astonied [astonished] at thee; his visage was so marred more than any man, and his form more than the sons of men:
So shall he sprinkle many nations; the kings shall shut their mouths at him: for *that* which had not been told them shall they see; and *that* which they had not heard shall they consider.

Verses 13 and 14 are in shocking contrast to each other. This is a figure of speech called *Antithesis*.[7] These two verses are two great extremes juxtaposed; set side by side forming a violent contrast to shock the mind. In verse 13 his glorification is the loftiest conceivable. But in verse 14 his degradation is the deepest possible. The height of his eminence and glorification is held in sharp, brutal contrast to the depth of his degradation and wretchedness.

Isaiah 53:1 and 2:
Who hath believed our report? and to whom is the arm of the LORD revealed?
For he shall grow up before him as a tender plant, and as a root out of a dry ground: he hath no form nor comeliness; and when we shall see him, *there is* no beauty that we should desire him.

---

[7] E.W. Bullinger, *Figures of Speech Used in the Bible* (Grand Rapids, Michigan: Baker Book House, 1968) 715.

Our Identification with Christ's Sacrifice

"Arm of the Lord revealed" refers to God fighting for his people. (Jeremiah 21:5). The Lord God now effects the salvation and redemption of his people. He fights for His people like never before. He presents the great sacrifice for all time, for all people, which will save them from their sins and sickness.

> Isaiah 53:3 and 4:
> He is despised and rejected of men; a man of sorrows, and acquainted with grief [sicknesses]: and we hid as it were *our* faces from him; he was despised, and we esteemed him not.
> Surely he hath **borne** our griefs [sicknesses], and **carried** our sorrows: yet we did esteem him stricken, smitten of God, and afflicted.

The various words in this chapter which refer to the substitution in Christ's sacrifice have been accented by bold print. The overarching point of this chapter is the identification the believers have with their substitute, the coming Messiah.

Now in precise detail verse four lays out what Jesus Christ's sacrifice accomplished. The word "grief" is the Hebrew word for sickness or disease. "Sorrow" is acute mental pain and anguish. As our substitute, he carried off our sickness and our heartache. All our ills, whether physical or mental, have been transferred to him. Verse four is quoted in Matthew 8:17. Spiritual deliverance and physical healing are ours by what Christ has accomplished.

> Isaiah 53:5:
> But he *was* wounded **for** our transgressions, *he was* bruised **for** our iniquities: the chastisement of our peace *was* **upon** him; and with his stripes we are healed.

"…The chastisement of our peace *was* upon him" should read, "the punishment was laid upon him for our peace." We have peace. Christ was our peace offering. Again here in verse five it mentions healing—the stripes laid on him have made us sound and well.

> Isaiah 53:6-9:
> All we like sheep have gone astray; we have turned every one to his own way; and the LORD hath **laid on** him the iniquity of us all.
> He was oppressed, and he was afflicted, yet he opened not his mouth: he is brought as a lamb to the slaughter, and as a sheep before her shearers is dumb, so he openeth not his mouth.
> He was taken from prison and from judgment: and who shall declare his generation? for he was cut off out of the land of the living: **for** the transgression of my people was he stricken.
> And he made his grave with the wicked, and with the rich in his death; because he had done no violence [wrong], neither *was any* deceit in his mouth.

These verses continue to specifically enumerate what the sacrifice of Christ will accomplish. Verse nine is another startling enigma: his death was dishonorable and held up for public disgrace; but, in contrast, his burial was prestigious, among the rich. Because of the believing of one man, Joseph of Arimathea, this prophecy was fulfilled.[8]

---

[8] Also see: Victor Paul Weirwille, *Jesus Christ, Our Passover* (New Knoxville, Ohio: American Christian Press, 1980) 266-272.

Jesus Christ, The Trespass Offering

In this prophecy of Isaiah there is noteworthy reference to one of the Levitical offerings.

> Isaiah 53:10:
> Yet it pleased the LORD to bruise him; he hath put *him* to grief: when thou shalt make his soul an offering for sin [*asham*, trespass offering], he shall see *his* seed, he shall prolong *his* days, and the pleasure of the LORD shall prosper in his hand.

"Offering for sin" is one word in the Hebrew: *asham*. This Hebrew word is usually translated "trespass offering." The trespass offering was one of the offerings of Leviticus 1-7. It was the only offering where there was a compensation paid to cover the offence or trespass of the offerer. If financial restitution was possible, the full amount was repaid and then one fifth was added. The main distinction of this offering was compensatory payment. The trespass offering canceled out the sin and then it included a full payment plus 20%.

Isaiah 53:10 declares the soul of the coming redeemer was made a trespass offering. This Levitical offering pointed toward Christ who would made full restitution. Jesus Christ not only paid off our trespasses, he added an extra 20% for compensatory damages! He is our trespass offering before God. All our debts and obligations before God have been paid, plus. All that Adam lost, Christ has restored and much more. Jesus Christ was a complete offering for us.

Isaiah 53:11 and 12:

He shall see of the travail of his soul, *and* shall be satisfied: by his knowledge shall my righteous servant justify many; for he shall **bear** their iniquities.

Therefore will I divide him *a portion* with the great, and he shall divide the spoil with the strong; because he hath poured out his soul unto death: and he was numbered with the transgressors; and he **bare** the sin of many, and made intercession for the transgressors.

It says "by his knowledge" in verse 11. That is the key to receiving the benefits into manifestation in your life. You must discern and understand exactly what Christ has accomplished on your behalf. Once you have the knowledge, continue to recognize with due appreciation what Christ has borne for you. Then you will tap into the mental and physical wholeness God has for you.

Appendix

Sources Outside the Scriptures

Eating Food Sacrificed an Idol indicates Identification with that Idol:

From these secular sources it can be seen that was commonly understood in ancient times that when one ate food sacrificed and dedicated to an idol one was spiritually identified and sharing with that idol.

S. Angus in *The Mystery Religions: A Study in the Religious Background of Early Christianity* (New York: Dover, 1975) p. 128, 129. (Originally published under the title, *The Mystery Religions and Christianity* in 1925):

> Sacred meals played an important part in the Mysteries [of pagan religion] as sacraments of union with the deity…
>
> An inscription from Kos has preserved and interesting ritual: "Aristides tells how the worshippers of Serapis [an idol] partake in the full communion with him by 'inviting him to the hearth as guest and host.'

As instances of the deity as host, we may cite the dinner-invitation of a second-century [B.C.?] papyrus, 'Chaeremon invites you to dine at the table of the Lord Serapis [idol], tomorrow, 15th, at nine o'clock...'

F. Cumont [French scholar] stated that:

The original significance of the eating of a sacred animal [which had been sacrificed] in the Phrygian cults [religious system] was that "it was believed that thus there took place an **identification** with the god himself, together with a participation in his substance and qualities." (emphasis added).

Gerd Theissen in The Social Setting of Pauline Christianity (Philadelphia: Fortress, 1975) p. 129, quoting ancient writer Aelius Aristides.

"Moreover, in sacrifices men maintain an especially close fellowship with this god alone. They call him to the sanctuary and install him as both guest of honor and host, so that while some divinities provide portions of their common meals, he is the sole provider of all common meals."

Laying hands on a sacrifice indicates Identification

Jacob Milgrom in *The Anchor Bible Leviticus 1-16* (Doubleday, New York, 1991) p. 1075 quotes from ancient Hittite sources and concludes that laying on of hand on the animal "reflects the establishment of **identification** between the animals and humans, meaning, 'These are our rams of appeasement, these are our substitutes...' (emphasis added).

Made in the USA
Columbia, SC
29 September 2024

43193974R00028